Dear Parents and Guardians,

Though children are widely shown uppercase letters at the beginning of their linguistic adventures, lowercase letters are what they will be more commonly exposed to in school. For this reason, I recommend that when working at home, you focus on the lowercase alphabet. Children will need to know their letter names, however *it is far more important to the development of reading skills that they know* letter sounds. Correctly associating letters with the sounds they make is a proven method to help young children learn to read.

Here are some tips for using this book to help your child to learn letter sounds. At the top of each page, name the letter you see, and then continue to read the word that goes with the picture on the page. Be sure to put emphasis on the beginning sound of each word, and also *isolate it* from the vowel or consonant that follows it. For example; n says /n/, not /nuh/, and r says /r/, not /ruh/. When you see a letter in the middle of two forward slashes, *say the letter sound*, rather than the letter name. The bottom of each page focuses on sound only. Repetition of the sound while looking at the letter, will help your child to make a solid connection.

I hope you enjoy this book, and that it creates fun, learning experiences for you and your child. This book is an introduction to some of the characters and settings of many adventures to come in The Magic Forest. More information can be found at www.littlegempublishing.org

Happy reading, *Audrey Walsh*

Now for the boring stuff:

No part of this publication may be reproduced, stored in a retrieval system, or transmitted in any form or by any means, electronic, mechanical, photocopying, recording or otherwise, without the expressed written permission of the publisher, except for brief quotations embodied in certain articles or reviews.

For more information, please contact
http://www.littlegempublishing.org

The Magic Forest™ Copyright © 2015 by Little Gem Publishing, LLC. All rights reserved.
ISBN-13: 978-1944291006 (Little Gem Publishing)
ISBN-10: 1944291008

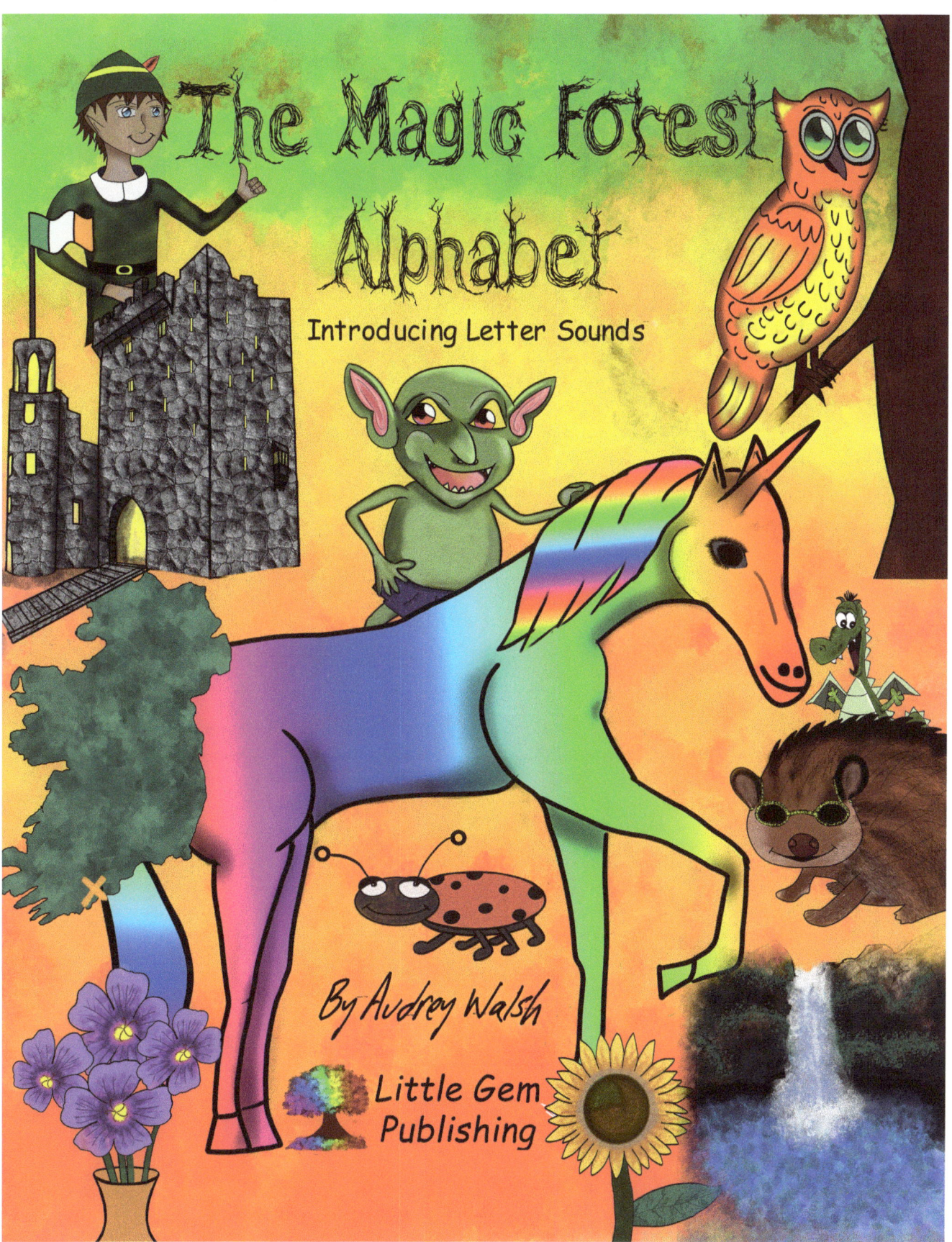

Gratitude

A special thank you to my sister, Cathy (Montessori kindergarten teacher extraordinaire), for her invaluable input. For my 6 yr old daughter, Lilly, my best critic, and my husband whose never-ending support and cheerleading made it all possible.

a is for apple

/a/ . . . /a/ . . . /a/pple

b is for butterfly

/b/ . . . /b/ . . . /b/utterfly

c is for castle

/c/ . . . /c/ . . . /c/astle

d is for dragon

/d/ . . . /d/ . . . /d/ragon

e is for elf

/e/ . . . /e/ . . . /e/lf

f is for frog

/f/ . . . /f/ . . . /f/rog

g is for goblin

/g/ . . . /g/ . . . /g/oblin

h is for hedgehog

/h/ . . . /h/ . . . /h/edgehog

i is for igloo

/i/ . . . /i/ . . . /i/gloo

j is for jug

/j/ . . . /j/ . . . /j/ug

k is for kitten

/k/ . . . /k/ . . . /k/itten

l is for ladybug

/l/ . . . /l/ . . . /l/adybug

m is for mermaid

/m/ . . . /m/ . . . /m/ermaid

n is for nest

/n/ . . . /n/ . . . /n/est

o is for octopus

/o/ . . . /o/ . . . /o/ctopus

p is for pond

/p/ . . . /p/ . . . /p/ond

q is for quill

/q/ . . . /q/ . . . /q/uill

r is for rainbow unicorn

/r/ . . . /r/ . . . /r/ainbow unicorn

s is for sunflower

/s/ . . . /s/ . . . /s/unflower

t is for tree

/t/ . . . /t/ . . . /t/ree

u is for umbrella

/u/ . . . /u/ . . . /u/mbrella

v is for violets

/v/ . . . /v/ . . . /v/iolets

w is for waterfall

/w/ . . . /w/ . . . /w/aterfall

x is x marks the spot

/x/ . . . /x/ . . ./x/ marks the spot

y is for yawn

/y/ . . . /y/ . . . /y/awn

z is for zoanthid coral

/z . . . /z/ . . . /z/oanthid coral

You can now practice putting sounds together with your child. For example,

/a/ /t/ . . . at
/o/ /n/ . . . on
/u/ /p/ . . . up
/a/ /m/ . . . am
/a/ /n/ /d/ . . . and
/g/ /o/ /t/ . . . got
/c/ /a/ /t/ . . . cat
/d/ /o/ /g/ . . . dog

Now review the words together.

at   and
on   got
up   cat
am   dog

Check out the latest news from The Magic Forest at www.littlegempublishing.org . So much more to come!!!

www.ingramcontent.com/pod-product-compliance
Lightning Source LLC
Chambersburg PA
CBHW051250110526
44588CB00025B/2946